popcorn treats

popcorn treats

delicious recipes for savoury snacks & sweet treats

Hannah Miles

photography by Tara Fisher

RYLAND
PETERS
& SMALL
LONDON NEW YORK

*for joshua & rosie,
my 'taste buds'*

Senior Designer Iona Hoyle
Editor Rebecca Woods
Production Laura Grundy
Art Director Leslie Harrington
Editorial Director Julia Charles

Prop Stylist Liz Belton
Food Stylist Annie Rigg
Indexer Hilary Bird

First published in 2012
by Ryland Peters & Small
20–21 Jockey's Fields
London WC1R 4BW
and
519 Broadway, 5th Floor
New York, NY 10012
www.rylandpeters.com

Text © Hannah Miles 2012
Design and photographs
© Ryland Peters & Small 2012
Printed in China

10 9 8 7 6 5 4 3 2 1

ISBN: 978-1-84975-200-8

A CIP record for this book is
available from the British Library.

US Library of Congress Cataloging-
in-publication data has been
applied for.

author's acknowledgments

With thanks, as always, to Ryland
Peters & Small for publishing
this fun book, to Julia Charles for
believing in my crazy popcorn
ideas and to Rebecca Woods for
the patient editing. Thanks to Iona
Hoyle for the wonderful design, to
Annie Rigg and Liz Belton for the
fun styling and Tara Fisher for the
wonderful photography. Particular
thanks to Amelia Champ from
Zaramama for the huge popcorn
inspiration and for the millions of
popcorn kernels that I ate during
the testing of this book – your
services to popcorn are legendary.
Particular thanks also to my
wonderful taste testers – Jess,
Miles, Mark, Katharine, Rosie, Lucy,
David, Steve, Pam, Toby, Jana, Josef,
Sacha, Alison, Apple and the ladies
of Podington Sewing Circle – I hope
the popcorn addiction wanes
sometime soon!

notes

• All spoon measurements are level,
unless otherwise specified.

• Ovens should be preheated to the
specified temperature. Recipes in
this book were tested using a
regular oven. If using a fan-assisted/
convection oven, follow the
manufacturer's instructions for
adjusting temperatures.

• All eggs are large, unless
otherwise specified.

• All recipes give directions for
popcorn made in a saucepan, but it
can also be prepared in a popcorn
maker, if you have one, or in the
microwave. If you are using a
microwave, be sure to use popcorn
specially packaged for microwave
cooking.

contents

getting ready to pop

popcorn – an all time cinema favourite and the latest trend in snack food! Whether you pop yours in a saucepan, popcorn machine or microwave, these delicious and healthy kernels can be adorned with a wide variety of flavours, both sweet and savoury, and are perfect for home cinema nights, lunch box snacks and homemade gifts. There is something about waiting for the kernels to pop in a pan that can't help but make you smile. People have been enjoying popcorn for many centuries and I've often wondered about the reaction of the first person to discover how to pop corn – it must have seemed almost magical that a delicious white puff of tastiness appeared from a dried hard corn kernel!

Popcorn can be prepared in many different ways. The recipes in this book provide instructions for cooking corn in a regular pan, but if you make a lot of popcorn you may wish to invest in a traditional popcorn pan, which has a paddle inside to ensure even cooking. You turn the handle while the corn is cooking which adds fun to the popping experience. Alternatively, electric popcorn machines are available to buy fairly cheaply. These produce really healthy popcorn as the kernels are popped using hot air rather than oil. The third way of cooking popcorn is in the microwave, but it is important to use popcorn that is specially packaged for microwave cooking and follow the instructions on the packet so your popcorn doesn't explode! Pop-a-cobs are also available where you pop a whole corn cob in the microwave in a microwave-proof bag – they are spectacular to watch as they pop.

Corn itself comes in a wide variety of types with many different sizes and flavours. From tiny kernels of baby corn, which produce a dainty crisp kernel, to coloured corn which gives a golden coloured popcorn. It is worth buying good quality corn as it has a superior flavour, although if you are covering your popcorn in a toffee or other highly flavoured coating, this is not essential. You need to take care – particularly when using popcorn in baked recipes, such as those in the Treats chapter – that you remove all unpopped kernels from the corn before using as these are hard and can be a hazard to your teeth.

When it comes to flavourings, popcorn really comes into its own. Undressed, these crispy puffs do not have a strong taste and while they are delicious plain, they are also the perfect vessel for your favourite flavour. I prefer sweet popcorn to salty, but there are many people who are the complete reverse – it is really a matter of personal taste. Whatever your preference, there is a popcorn recipe in this book for you – from spicy Thai and Indian flavoured kernels to sweet honeycomb or gourmet salted caramel. There are even a few quirky varieties, such as popcorn flavoured with your favourite alcoholic tipples – Bloody Mary and Margarita.

There are many ways to serve popcorn – in large bowls, perfect for sharing, or individual servings in classic striped bags, ideal for a lunchbox treat. Retro cinema popcorn boxes can be bought online and are a great way to serve your popcorn while watching a movie at home. If giving as a gift, you can pack popcorn in small bags tied with colourful ribbons or seal them in airtight containers such as Kilner or Weck jars. During the festive season you could even thread popcorn onto long cotton threads using a sharp needle and use as garlands to decorate the Christmas tree.

The possibilities for this tasty treat are endless. So whichever great flavour takes your fancy, get popping today!

Sweet

Caramel popcorn is an all time favourite. Although there are popular versions available to buy in the shops, nothing quite beats the flavour of homemade warm toffee popcorn with a creamy buttery toffee sauce coating every popped kernel.

butter toffee popcorn

Heat the oil in a large lidded saucepan with a few popcorn kernels in the pan. When you hear the kernels pop, carefully tip in the rest of the kernels. Shake the pan over the heat until the popping stops. Take care when lifting the lid as any unpopped kernels may still pop from the heat of the pan. Tip the popcorn into a bowl, removing any unpopped kernels as you go.

Put the butter, sugar, syrup, vanilla extract and salt in a small saucepan and simmer gently, stirring frequently, until the butter has melted and the sugar has dissolved. You should be left with a thick toffee sauce.

Pour the warm toffee sauce over the popcorn, stirring well so that the popcorn is evenly coated. Serve either warm or cold, but if eating cold, make sure that you stir the popcorn every 20 minutes or so as it cools to prevent it sticking together.

1–2 tablespoons sunflower or vegetable oil

90 g/⅓ cup popcorn kernels

70 g/5 tablespoons butter

100 g/½ cup packed brown sugar

60 ml/¼ cup golden syrup/light corn syrup

1 teaspoon vanilla extract

a pinch of sea salt

makes 1 large bowl

I took this popcorn to our village sewing circle with some other popcorn samples and it was the first bowl to empty. The tang of raspberry is tamed by the creaminess of the smooth white chocolate, making it a truly delicious treat.

raspberry & white chocolate popcorn

1–2 tablespoons sunflower or vegetable oil

90 g/⅓ cup popcorn kernels

100 g/6½ tablespoons butter

1 teaspoon vanilla extract

15 g/2 tablespoons freeze dried raspberry powder ✳

100 g/½ cup white chocolate chips

makes 1 large bowl

Heat the oil in a large lidded saucepan with a few popcorn kernels in the pan. When you hear the kernels pop, carefully tip in the rest of the kernels. Shake the pan over the heat until the popping stops. Take care when lifting the lid as any unpopped kernels may pop from the heat of the pan. Tip the popcorn into a bowl, removing any unpopped kernels as you go.

Melt the butter in a small saucepan and add the vanilla extract.

Pour the butter over the popcorn and stir well so that it evenly coats the popcorn. Sprinkle over the raspberry powder and stir in the white chocolate chips while the popcorn is still warm so that the chocolate melts into the popcorn. This popcorn can be eaten warm or cold.

✳tip Freeze dried raspberry powder is available from health food shops and online. However, if you cannot find any, you can make your own by drying raspberries in an oven set to a very low temperature for about 6–8 hours, or in a dehumidifier, and then blitzing them to a fine powder in a blender.

Zaramama, Queen of Popcorn, was a great source of inspiration for this book. Her wonderfully coloured popcorn kernels and pop-a-cobs are too good to resist. She very kindly shared her recipe for peanut butter popcorn with me, which has been fine-tuned over many years! If you are a fan of Reese's pieces and like a peanut chocolate fix, sprinkle a handful of dark chocolate chips or Reese's pieces into the mix.

zaramama's peanut butter popcorn

Heat the oil in a large lidded saucepan with a few popcorn kernels in the pan. When you hear the kernels pop, carefully tip in the rest of the kernels. Shake the pan over the heat until the popping stops. Take care when lifting the lid as any unpopped kernels may pop from the heat of the pan. Tip the popcorn into a bowl, removing any unpopped kernels as you go.

Put the peanut butter, butter, sugar and vanilla extract in a small saucepan and heat until the butter has melted and the sugar has dissolved, stirring all the time so the sauce does not stick.

Pour the peanut butter sauce over the popcorn and stir well so that the popcorn is evenly coated. Tip in the peanuts and stir again to mix through. Serve warm or cold.

1–2 tablespoons sunflower or vegetable oil

90 g/$\frac{1}{3}$ cup popcorn kernels

170 g/$\frac{1}{4}$ cup peanut butter (smooth or crunchy)

80 g/5$\frac{1}{2}$ tablespoons butter

50 g/$\frac{1}{4}$ cup sugar

1 teaspoon vanilla extract

100 g/$\frac{3}{4}$ cup honey roasted peanuts

makes 1 large bowl

Vanilla pods are a luxury as they are quite expensive to buy. They are taken from the vanilla orchid plant, which has to be pollinated by hand, hence the cost, with the best varieties coming from Madagascar and India. This popcorn may be simple but the vanilla flavour is delicious and irresistible. Dark vanilla seeds pepper the butter sauce giving the popcorn a heady aroma.

vanilla popcorn

1–2 tablespoons sunflower
or vegetable oil
90 g/⅓ cup popcorn kernels
1 vanilla pod/bean ✳
80 g/5½ tablespoons butter
70 g/⅓ cup caster/superfine sugar

makes 1 large bowl

Heat the oil in a large lidded saucepan with a few popcorn kernels in the pan. When you hear the kernels pop, carefully tip in the rest of the kernels. Shake the pan over the heat until the popping stops. Take care when lifting the lid as any unpopped kernels may still pop from the heat of the pan. Tip the popcorn into a bowl, removing any unpopped kernels as you go.

Split the vanilla pod lengthways and remove the seeds by running a round bladed knife along both halves of the pod. Add the pod halves and seeds to a small saucepan with the butter and heat gently, stirring, until the butter has melted.

Remove the vanilla pod from the pan and pour the vanilla butter over the popcorn. (Reserve the vanilla pod as it can be reused following the tip below.) Sprinkle over the sugar and stir well so that everything is evenly coated. This popcorn is delicious warm or cold.

✳tip If you don't have a vanilla pod available, you can substitute vanilla sugar for the caster/superfine sugar in this recipe or add a few teaspoons of vanilla bean paste or extract to the butter. There is still a lot of flavour in the discarded vanilla pod. Wash and dry it, then place in a jar filled with sugar and leave for three weeks to make your own vanilla infused sugar.

This is a delicious popcorn, flavoured with melted chocolate and pieces of honeycomb.
It is very simple to prepare, allowing you to whip up a delicious sweet treat in no time at all.
I find it one of those addictive popcorns, where you just can't stop eating and then all of
a sudden the bowl is empty — you have been warned!

honeycomb popcorn

Heat the oil in a large lidded saucepan with a few popcorn kernels in the pan. When you hear the kernels pop, carefully tip in the rest of the kernels. Shake the pan over the heat until the popping stops. Take care when lifting the lid as any unpopped kernels may still pop from the heat of the pan. Tip the popcorn into a bowl, removing any unpopped kernels as you go.

Crush the chocolate-covered honeycomb into small pieces. If you are using wrapped bars, you can crush them by tapping them firmly with a rolling pin before unwrapping. If you have loose honeycomb pieces, put them in a clean, plastic freezer bag wrapped in a clean dish towel and tap firmly with a rolling pin until broken into small pieces.

Sprinkle the honeycomb and chocolate chips over the still warm popcorn and stir through so that the chocolate melts and sticks the honeycomb pieces to the popcorn. This popcorn can be served warm or cold.

1–2 tablespoons sunflower or vegetable oil

90 g/⅓ cup popcorn kernels

160 g/5½ oz. chocolate-covered honeycomb (such as Crunchie or Butterfinger bars)

50 g/¼ cup milk chocolate chips

makes 1 large bowl

If you like bananas then this is the popcorn for you. Sticky maple syrup popcorn, coated in banana dust and served with whole dried banana chips. This popcorn is delicious served warm and freshly made.

banana maple popcorn

200 g/2 cups dried banana chips

1–2 tablespoons sunflower or vegetable oil

90 g/⅓ cup popcorn kernels

80 g/5½ tablespoons butter

80 ml/⅓ cup pure maple syrup

makes 1 large bowl

Put 120 g/1 generous cup of the banana chips in a food processor and blitz to a fine powder.

Heat the oil in a large lidded saucepan with a few popcorn kernels in the pan. When you hear the kernels pop, carefully tip in the rest of the kernels. Shake the pan over the heat until the popping stops. Take care when lifting the lid as any unpopped kernels may still pop from the heat of the pan. Tip the popcorn into a bowl, removing any unpopped kernels as you go.

Put the butter and maple syrup in a small saucepan and heat gently, stirring, until the butter has melted.

Pour the maple butter over the popcorn, sprinkle over the banana powder and the remaining whole banana chips and stir well so that all the popcorn is evenly coated. This popcorn is best served warm.

Sweet long shredded coconut is delicious when toasted. Paired with a light coating of melted extra virgin coconut oil, this popcorn has a tropical flavour. You could even add a drizzle of coconut rum for an extra special treat.

coconut popcorn

In a small heavy-based frying pan, dry roast the shredded coconut, stirring constantly, until it starts to colour and give off a nutty aroma. It is important to keep moving it around the pan as coconut can burn very easily. Remove from the pan, tip onto a plate and set aside.

Heat the oil in a large lidded saucepan with a few popcorn kernels in the pan. When you hear the kernels pop, carefully tip in the rest of the kernels. Shake the pan over the heat until the popping stops. Take care when lifting the lid as any unpopped kernels may still pop from the heat of the pan. Tip the popcorn into a bowl, removing any unpopped kernels as you go.

Put the coconut oil in a small saucepan and heat gently, stirring, until it has melted.

Pour the melted coconut oil over the popcorn, sprinkle over the toasted coconut and sugar and stir well until all the popcorn is evenly coated. This popcorn can be served warm or cold.

100 g/1 cup long soft long shredded coconut

1–2 tablespoons sunflower or vegetable oil

90 g/$\frac{1}{3}$ cup popcorn kernels

100 g/6 tablespoons extra virgin coconut oil

60 g/$\frac{1}{3}$ cup caster/superfine sugar

makes 1 large bowl

savoury

This popcorn is simple but very tasty. The amount of salt and pepper to add is very much down to personal taste, so add gradually and keep tasting until you are happy. Tiny popcorn kernels are ideal to use as they are delicate and hold the salt and pepper grains well.

Salt & pepper popcorn

1–2 tablespoons sunflower or vegetable oil

90 g/⅓ cup mini popcorn kernels

sea salt and freshly ground black pepper

makes 1 large bowl

Heat the oil in a large lidded saucepan with a few popcorn kernels in the pan. When you hear the kernels pop, carefully tip in the rest of the kernels. Shake the pan over the heat until the popping stops. Take care when lifting the lid as any unpopped kernels may still pop from the heat of the pan. Tip the popcorn into a bowl, removing any unpopped kernels as you go.

Season the popcorn well with salt and pepper (about a teaspoon of each is about right for me) and serve warm or cold.

Smoky bacon crisps were always popular when we were children and are the inspiration for this tasty popcorn, flavoured with homemade bacon powder and lots of smoky paprika. For an indulgent treat you could also add some grated cheese while the popcorn is still hot so it melts over the top.

paprika smoky bacon popcorn

In a food processor, blitz the crispy smoked bacon pieces/real bacon bits to a fine powder and set aside.

Heat the oil in a large lidded saucepan with a few popcorn kernels in the pan. When you hear the kernels pop, carefully tip in the rest of the kernels. Shake the pan over the heat until the popping stops. Take care when lifting the lid as any unpopped kernels may still pop from the heat of the pan. Tip the popcorn into a bowl, removing any unpopped kernels as you go.

Melt the butter in a small saucepan set over medium heat and then pour over the warm popcorn. Sprinkle over the bacon powder and paprika and stir well so the popcorn is evenly coated. Season to taste with black pepper. Add the cheese, if using, while the popcorn is still warm so that it melts onto the popcorn. Serve warm or cold.

50 g/½ cup crispy smoked bacon pieces/real bacon bits

1–2 tablespoons sunflower or vegetable oil

90 g/⅓ cup popcorn kernels

60 g/5 tablespoons butter

2 teaspoons smoked Spanish paprika (pimentón)

freshly ground black pepper

50 g/⅓ cup grated Cheddar cheese, to serve (optional)

makes 1 large bowl

This recipe transports you to the bustling markets of India where popcorn is served as a popular street food. Flavoured with spices of the orient, delicious sweet and sour pickle and chutney, and rich ghee, this is a great nibble to serve with drinks before dinner.

bombay popcorn

1–2 tablespoons sunflower or vegetable oil

90 g/⅓ cup popcorn kernels

60 g/5 tablespoons ghee (clarified butter)

1 tablespoon onion/nigella seeds

1 tablespoon dried curry leaves

1 generous tablespoon lime pickle

1 generous tablespoon mango chutney

makes 1 large bowl

Heat the oil in a large lidded saucepan with a few popcorn kernels in the pan. When you hear the kernels pop, carefully tip in the rest of the kernels. Shake the pan over the heat until the popping stops. Take care when lifting the lid as any unpopped kernels may still pop from the heat of the pan. Tip the popcorn into a bowl, removing any unpopped kernels as you go.

Melt the ghee in a small saucepan set over low heat. Add the onion/nigella seeds and curry leaves and cook for a few minutes to flavour the oil. Add the pickle and chutney and cook for a few more minutes to heat through.

Pour the spiced ghee over the popcorn and stir well so that the kernels are evenly coated. Serve warm or cold.

It may seem strange to add sugar to savoury popcorn, but it really brings out the flavour of the chilli and softens the heat slightly. The number of chillies will depend on how hot you like your food — one will be a fairly mild heat, three will be very spicy.

chilli popcorn

Heat the oil in a large lidded saucepan with a few popcorn kernels in the pan. When you hear the kernels pop, carefully tip in the rest of the kernels. Shake the pan over the heat until the popping stops. Take care when lifting the lid as any unpopped kernels may still pop from the heat of the pan. Tip the popcorn into a bowl, removing any unpopped kernels as you go.

Grind the salt, chillies and sugar in a mortar and pestle until the chillies are completely broken down to a fine dust. Sprinkle the chilli mix over the popcorn and squeeze over a little lime juice to bring out the flavour. Stir well so that the popcorn is evenly coated and serve warm or cold.

1–2 tablespoons sunflower or vegetable oil

90 g/⅓ cup popcorn kernels

1 teaspoon salt

1–3 small dried bird's eye chillies

2 teaspoons caster/superfine sugar

freshly squeezed juice of 1 lime

makes 1 large bowl

I love the flavours of Thai cuisine – sharp limes, fragrant curry leaves, chilli and lemongrass. Whilst you can make your own Thai green curry paste, there are several excellent varieties you can buy in supermarkets and it certainly saves a lot of time and effort. Ready-made pastes vary in strength so you may need to reduce the quantity added if you have a very strongly flavoured paste.

thai spiced popcorn

100 g/6 tablespoons extra virgin coconut oil, plus 1–2 tablespoons for cooking the popcorn

90 g/⅓ cup popcorn kernels

1 tablespoon Thai green curry paste

1 teaspoon lemongrass puree ✳

grated zest from 1 unwaxed lime

2 teaspoons sugar

1 generous tablespoon finely chopped fresh coriander/cilantro

sea salt and freshly ground black pepper

makes 1 large bowl

Heat 1–2 tablespoons of coconut oil in a large lidded saucepan with a few popcorn kernels in the pan. When you hear the kernels pop, carefully tip in the rest of the kernels. Shake the pan over the heat until the popping stops. Take care when lifting the lid as any unpopped kernels may pop from the heat of the pan. Tip the popcorn into a bowl, removing any unpopped kernels as you go.

Melt the remaining extra virgin coconut oil in a small saucepan set over low heat. Add the curry paste, lemongrass purée and lime zest and cook for a few minutes, stirring all the time.

Pour the Thai-flavoured coconut oil over the warm popcorn, sprinkle with the sugar, coriander/cilantro, salt and pepper, and stir well so that the popcorn is evenly coated. This popcorn can be eaten warm or cold.

✳tip Lemongrass purée is available in most supermarkets, but if you are unable to find it you can substitute a 2-cm/1-inch piece of lemongrass, finely chopped and pounded in a mortar and pestle with 1 tablespoon of vegetable oil.

Pumpkin seed oil is such a treat — it has an amazing flavour and is perfect for cooking popcorn as it gives the kernels a delicious taste and a vibrant green colour. Served with toasted pumpkin seeds and freshly ground salt and pepper, this popcorn is a delicious yet healthy snack.

pumpkin seed popcorn

Heat the oil in a large lidded saucepan with a few popcorn kernels in the pan. When you hear the kernels pop, carefully tip in the rest of the kernels. Shake the pan over the heat until the popping stops. Take care when lifting the lid as any unpopped kernels may pop from the heat of the pan. Stir the popcorn well so that it is evenly coated in the oil, drizzling over a little more oil if necessary. Tip the popcorn into a bowl, removing any unpopped kernels as you go.

Sprinkle the toasted pumpkin seeds over the popcorn, season with a good crunch of salt and pepper (about a teaspoon of each is right for me) and stir well. Serve warm or cold.

3–4 tablespoons pumpkin seed oil, plus extra for drizzling

90 g/⅓ cup popcorn kernels

5 tablespoons toasted pumpkin seeds

sea salt and freshly ground black pepper

makes 1 large bowl

This popcorn dish is a twist on the classic tortilla nachos. With delicious avocado tomato salsa flavoured with paprika, basil and coriander, finished with sour cream and topped with bubbling melted cheese, these make the perfect movie night snack for sharing.

popcorn nachos

1–2 tablespoons sunflower or vegetable oil

50 g/2 tablespoons popcorn kernels

for the avocado salsa
2 beef/beefsteak tomatoes

1 small shallot, finely chopped

2 ripe avocados, peeled, pitted and chopped

freshly squeezed juice of 1 lime

1 tablespoon finely chopped fresh basil

2 tablespoons finely chopped fresh coriander/cilantro

1 teaspoon hot paprika

1 teaspoon caster/superfine sugar

sea salt and freshly ground black pepper

to serve
150 ml/⅔ cup sour cream

100 g/¾ cup grated Cheddar cheese

serves 4–6

Heat the oil in a large lidded saucepan with a few popcorn kernels in the pan. When you hear the kernels pop, carefully tip in the rest of the kernels. Shake the pan over the heat until the popping stops. Take care when lifting the lid as any unpopped kernels may still pop from the heat of the pan. Tip the popcorn into a serving dish, removing any unpopped kernels as you go.

To make the salsa, cut the tomatoes in half and discard the seeds and juice. Chop the tomato flesh into small pieces and put in a bowl with the chopped shallot, avocado and the lime juice. Stir so that the avocado is thoroughly coated in the lime juice (this will prevent discolouration). Add the chopped basil and coriander/cilantro, paprika and sugar, season well with salt and pepper and stir again. Drain the salsa in a sieve/strainer to remove any excess liquid.

Make a well in the popcorn and pour the salsa into the centre of the dish. Top with sour cream and sprinkle with the grated cheese. Place under a hot grill/broiler for about 5 minutes until the cheese melts and is bubbling, taking care that the popcorn does not burn. Remove from the grill/broiler and serve immediately.

treats

Chocolate crispy cakes are quick and easy to prepare yet taste divine. This recipe replaces some of the traditional cornflakes with popcorn, giving a lighter texture. Sprinkle the cakes with popping candy and these popcorn cakes will literally pop in the mouth as you tuck in.

popping popcorn crispy cakes

1–2 tablespoons sunflower or vegetable oil

50 g/3 tablespoons popcorn kernels

50 g/3½ tablespoons butter

125 ml/½ cup golden syrup/light corn syrup

150 g/5 oz. milk chocolate, broken into chunks

50 g/1 cup cornflakes

popping candy/space dust

coloured sprinkles or chocolate curls, to decorate

14 cupcake cases

makes 14

Heat the oil in a large lidded saucepan with a few popcorn kernels in the pan. When you hear the kernels pop, carefully tip in the rest of the kernels. Shake the pan over the heat until the popping stops. Take care when lifting the lid as any unpopped kernels may pop from the heat of the pan. Tip the popcorn into a mixing bowl, removing any unpopped kernels as you go.

Put the butter and syrup in a small saucepan and heat gently until the butter has melted. Add the chocolate and continue to heat, stirring constantly, until it has melted and you have a thick glossy sauce.

Add the cornflakes to the mixing bowl with the popcorn and pour over the warm chocolate sauce. Stir well with a wooden spoon making sure that everything is evenly coated.

Spoon the mixture into the cupcake cases. Sprinkle each cake with a little popping candy and decorate with sprinkles or chocolate curls. Leave to set before serving.

These delicious cookies, with hints of lemon and chocolate and a crunch of popcorn, will disappear from the plate as soon as they are served. They are quite simply irresistible and are the perfect accompaniment to a glass of ice cold milk.

popcorn cookies

Preheat the oven to 180°C (350°F) Gas 4.

Sift the flour and bicarbonate of soda/baking soda into a large mixing bowl and stir in the lemon zest and sugar.

Heat the butter and golden syrup/light corn syrup in a heavy-based saucepan until the butter has melted. Pour the butter over the flour and mix together with a wooden spoon. Allow to cool for a few minutes then beat in the egg and cream cheese. Stir in the chocolate chunks, macadamia nuts and popcorn and then bring the dough together with your hands.

Place small mounds of cookie dough (about the size of a large walnut) onto the prepared baking sheets. Leave a little space between them as they will spread during cooking. Press each cookie down with your fingers, then bake in the preheated oven for 10–15 minutes until golden brown on top but still slightly soft in the middle.

Remove from the oven and allow to cool on the baking sheets for a few minutes, then transfer to a wire rack to cool completely.

These cookies will keep for up to 5 days in an airtight container.

350 g/2⅔ cups self-raising flour

1 teaspoon bicarbonate of soda/ baking soda

grated zest of 1 unwaxed lemon

160 g/¾ cup caster/granulated sugar

125 g/1 stick butter

60 ml/¼ cup golden syrup/light corn syrup

1 egg

35 g/2½ tablespoons cream cheese

200 g/6½ oz. white chocolate, chopped

100 g/¾ cup macadamia nuts, halved

60 g/2 oz. caramel-coated popcorn (such as Butterkist)

2 baking sheets, greased and lined with baking parchment

makes 20

Ice cream sundaes are a favourite treat and this one, packed with toffee popcorn, popcorn flavoured ice cream and warm toffee sauce, will not disappoint. You can prepare the ice cream and toffee sauce in advance so these sundaes just need a quick assembly before serving.

popcorn sundae

for the ice cream
300 ml/1¼ cups double/heavy cream
300 ml/1¼ cups milk
90 g/3 oz. caramel-coated popcorn (such as Butterkist)
60 g/5 tablespoons sugar
5 egg yolks

for the toffee sauce
120 g/⅔ cup sugar
60 g/4 tablespoons butter
125 ml/½ cup double/heavy cream

to assemble
150–200 ml/⅔–¾ cup double/heavy cream
30 g/1 oz. caramel-coated popcorn (such as Butterkist)

ice cream maker (optional)

2 large or 4 small sundae glasses

serves 2—4

To make the ice cream, put the cream, milk and popcorn in a heavy-based saucepan and bring to the boil. Remove from the heat and set aside to infuse for 30 minutes.

Meanwhile, whisk the sugar and egg yolks together in a large mixing bowl for about 5 minutes until very pale and creamy.

Strain the infused cream mixture through a fine sieve/strainer, pressing down on the popcorn to release all the cream. Discard the popcorn pulp. Return the cream to the pan and bring to the boil, stirring all the time.

Pour the hot cream onto the eggs in a thin drizzle, whisking all the time. Return to the saucepan and heat for a few minutes until the custard starts to thicken. Set aside to cool.

Freeze in an ice cream maker following the manufacturer's instructions or in a freezer-proof container, whisking every 30 minutes to break up the ice crystals and returning to the freezer between whisking, until the ice cream is set.

To prepare the toffee sauce, put the sugar and butter in a small saucepan set over gentle heat and heat until the butter and sugar have melted and the caramel starts to turn golden brown. Pour in the cream gradually, stirring all the time, until you have a smooth caramel sauce. Pass through a fine mesh sieve/strainer to remove any sugar crystals, then set aside to cool.

When you are ready to serve, whip the cream to stiff peaks. Layer scoops of ice cream, whipped cream, toffee sauce and popcorn in sundae glasses. For a hot caramel sundae, warm the toffee sauce before drizzling over the sundae. Serve immediately.

Kids love lollipops and these delicious popcorn-mallow ones are sure to make them smile. They take no time at all to prepare and can be decorated with pretty coloured sprinkles, if you wish.

popcorn lollipops

Heat the oil in a large lidded saucepan with a few popcorn kernels in the pan. When you hear the kernels pop, carefully tip in the rest of the kernels. Shake the pan over the heat until the popping stops. Take care when lifting the lid as any unpopped kernels may still pop from the heat of the pan. Tip the popcorn into a bowl, removing any unpopped kernels as you go.

Heat the marshmallows and butter in a saucepan set over gentle heat, stirring all the time, until both have melted. Take care that the mixture does not burn. Pour over the popcorn and stir through so that every kernel is evenly coated. Leave to cool for 20 minutes.

Dust your hands with icing/confectioners' sugar (this will help prevent the marshmallow sticking to them) and shape the mixture into 10 balls about the size of a clementine or small orange. Place the balls on a silicon mat or sheet of baking parchment and insert a lollipop/popsicle stick into each. Sprinkle each lollipop with sugar sprinkles, if using, and leave to set for several hours before serving.

1–2 tablespoons sunflower or vegetable oil

50 g/3 tablespoons popcorn kernels

200 g/4 cups marshmallows

40 g/3 tablespoons butter

icing/confectioners' sugar, for dusting

sugar sprinkles (optional)

silicon mat or baking parchment

10 lollipop/popsicle sticks

makes 10

This recipe is a twist on the popular family favourite dessert banoffee pie, with lashings of cream, caramel and banana. Caramel-covered popcorn works best as the coating prevents the popcorn from going soft. I use chocolate caramel biscuits for the base as they give a delicious texture and flavour but you could use plain digestives or graham crackers if you prefer.

popcorn pie

300 g/10 oz. chocolate caramel digestive biscuits or chocolate-covered graham crackers

100 g/6½ tablespoons butter

3 ripe bananas

freshly squeezed juice of 1 lemon

400 g/1⅔ cups dulce de leche (thick caramel sauce)

90 g/3 oz. caramel-coated popcorn (such as Butterkist)

300 ml/1¼ cups double/heavy cream

to decorate

1 tablespoon grated dark chocolate

15 g/2 tablespoons caramel-coated popcorn (such as Butterkist)

1 tablespoon dried banana chips, broken into small pieces

20-cm/8-inch springform tin/pan, greased and lined with baking parchment

serves 8–10

In a food processor, blitz the digestive biscuits/graham crackers to fine crumbs then transfer them to a mixing bowl.

Melt the butter in a small saucepan, then pour over the biscuit/graham cracker crumbs and stir well. (The warm butter will melt the caramel and chocolate in the crumbs.) Spoon the buttery crumbs into the prepared tin/pan and press down firmly with the back of a large spoon.

Peel and cut the bananas into thick rings and put in a bowl. Pour over the lemon juice, toss gently so that the banana is coated in the juice (this will prevent the banana turning brown), then drain away any excess juice. Arrange the banana slices over the crumb base, spoon over the dulce de leche and sprinkle over the popcorn.

Whip the cream to stiff peaks, taking care not to over whip as the cream will curdle. Using a spatula, spread the cream evenly over the top of the pie. Sprinkle the top of the pie with the grated chocolate, remaining popcorn and dried banana chips. Chill in the fridge for 2 hours before serving. This pie is best eaten on the day it is made.

This delicious chocolate tiffin slice is packed with light popcorn, juicy cherries and chewy marshmallows. With milk, dark and white chocolate these tiny morsels are a choco-a-holic's dream. You only need to serve small squares as the slice is very rich.

rocky road popcorn slice

Heat the oil in a large lidded saucepan with a few popcorn kernels in the pan. When you hear the kernels pop, carefully tip in the rest of the kernels. Shake the pan over the heat until the popping stops. Take care when lifting the lid as any unpopped kernels may still pop from the heat of the pan. Tip the popcorn into a bowl, removing any unpopped kernels as you go.

In a heavy-based frying pan, dry roast the shredded coconut, stirring all the time, until it starts to colour and give off a nutty aroma. Tip onto a plate and set aside to cool.

Melt the milk and dark chocolate and butter in a large heatproof bowl set over a saucepan of barely simmering water, making sure that the base of the bowl does not touch the water. Stir the mixture to melt any lumps then remove the bowl from the pan, taking care as it will be hot, and leave to cool for about 10 minutes.

Add the popcorn, toasted coconut, marshmallows and cherries to the cooled chocolate mixture and stir well so that everything is evenly coated. Spoon the mixture into the prepared tin/pan and press out flat with the back of a spoon.

Melt the white chocolate in a heatproof bowl set over a pan of barely simmering water, and drizzle over the top of the tiffin slice. Decorate with sugar sprinkles, if using. Chill in the fridge for 2 hours until set, then cut into 24 small squares and serve.

1 tablespoon sunflower or vegetable oil

30 g/2 tablespoons popcorn kernels

30 g/1 oz. long soft shredded coconut (such as Baker's Edge)

100 g/3½ oz. milk chocolate, chopped

100 g/3½ oz. dark chocolate, chopped

65 g/4½ tablespoons butter

100 g/2 cups marshmallows, quartered

150 g/5 oz (about 1 cup) glacé/candied cherries

for the topping
75 g/2½ oz. white chocolate

sugar sprinkles (optional)

18 x 28-cm/7 x 11-inch deep rectangular cake tin/pan, greased and lined with baking parchment

makes 24

These little cakes are the perfect celebration of all things popcorn — the caramel popcorn flavoured sponges are topped with toffee buttercream, popcorn and a drizzle of warm caramel sauce. Use brightly coloured cupcake cases for a pretty effect.

popcorn cupcakes

for the toffee sauce
100 g/½ cup caster/granulated sugar

40 g/3 tablespoons butter

80 ml/⅓ cup double/heavy cream

for the cupcake batter
60 g/2 oz. caramel-coated popcorn (such as Butterkist)

115 g/1 stick butter, softened

115 g/½ cup plus 1 tablespoon caster/granulated sugar

2 eggs

115 g/1 scant cup self-raising flour, sifted

2 tablespoons crème fraîche or sour cream

for the topping
200 g/1⅓ cups icing /confectioners' sugar

2 tablespoons crème fraîche or sour cream

60 g/4 tablespoons butter, softened

60 g/2 oz. caramel-coated popcorn (such as Butterkist)

12-hole muffin tin/pan lined with cupcake cases

a piping bag fitted with a large star nozzle/tip

makes 12

Preheat the oven to 180°C (350°F) Gas 4.

To make the toffee sauce, put the sugar and butter in a small saucepan and whisk over gentle heat until the butter has melted, the sugar dissolved and the caramel starts to turn golden brown. Pour in the cream gradually, stirring all the time, until you have a smooth caramel sauce. Do not overcook the sauce once the cream is added as it will become too thick. If this happens, simply add a little more cream to the pan and stir again. Pass the sauce through a fine mesh sieve/strainer to remove any sugar crystals, then set aside to cool.

For the cupcake batter, blitz the caramel popcorn to a fine powder in a food processor. Put the butter and sugar in a large mixing bowl and beat together with a hand or electric whisk until light and creamy. Add the eggs and whisk again. Add the flour, crème fraîche, popcorn powder and 2 tablespoons of the cooled toffee sauce, and fold together using a large spoon or spatula. Spoon the batter into the muffin cases and bake in the preheated oven for 15–20 minutes, until the cakes are golden brown and spring back to the touch. Transfer to a wire rack to cool.

For the frosting, sift the icing/confectioners' sugar into a large bowl and add the crème fraîche, butter and 2 tablespoons of the cooled toffee sauce. Whisk together until light and creamy. Spoon into the piping bag and pipe a swirl of frosting on each cupcake. Top each cupcake with a few kernels of caramel popcorn and drizzle over the remaining toffee sauce. If you are serving the cakes straight away, you may want to reheat the toffee sauce slightly and pour it warm over the cakes for an extra special treat.

gourmet

Cinnamon and apple — the true flavours of autumn — are combined in this popcorn for a warming treat. You need to make sure that you reduce the apple juice to a syrup so that you have an intense apple flavour but the popcorn doesn't become soggy.

cinnamon apple popcorn

Heat the oil in a large lidded saucepan with a few popcorn kernels in the pan. When you hear the kernels pop, carefully tip in the rest of the kernels. Shake the pan over the heat until the popping stops. Take care when lifting the lid as any unpopped kernels may still pop from the heat of the pan. Tip the popcorn into a bowl, removing any unpopped kernels as you go.

For the apple syrup, pour the apple juice into a small saucepan set over medium heat and simmer until it has reduced to about 50 ml/¼ cup – this should take about 15 minutes. Add the butter to the pan and simmer, stirring, until the butter has all melted.

Pour the apple butter over the popcorn and stir thoroughly so that the popcorn is evenly coated. Sprinkle over the chopped apple, cinnamon and sugar and stir again. This popcorn can be served warm or cold.

1–2 tablespoons sunflower or vegetable oil

90 g/⅓ cup popcorn kernels

for the apple syrup
400 ml/1¾ cups cloudy apple juice

80 g/5½ tablespoons butter

to serve
80 g/3 oz. dried apple rings, finely chopped

2 generous teaspoons ground cinnamon

2 tablespoons caster/superfine sugar

makes 1 large bowl

This popcorn is inspired by the delicious hot sugar nuts that are available to buy at fairs and Christmas markets. I am unable to pass one of those stalls without stopping to buy them — the aroma of the hot caramel is simply irresistible. This popcorn keeps well as it is a dry popcorn. Perfect for lunchboxes or picnics, it is a true nut-a-holic's delight.

nutty popcorn

1–2 tablespoons sunflower or vegetable oil

90 g/⅓ cup popcorn kernels

for the caramel nuts
225 g/1 cup caster/superfine sugar

2 teaspoons vanilla extract

250 g/8 oz. mixed roasted nuts✳ (such as pecans, peanuts, almonds, macadamias)

makes 1 large bowl

Heat the oil in a large lidded saucepan with a few popcorn kernels in the pan. When you hear the kernels pop, carefully tip in the rest of the kernels. Shake the pan over the heat until the popping stops. Take care when lifting the lid as any unpopped kernels may still pop from the heat of the pan. Tip the popcorn into a bowl, removing any unpopped kernels as you go.

To make the caramel nuts, put the sugar, vanilla extract and 125 ml/½ cup water in a small saucepan set over medium heat. Simmer until the sugar dissolves and you have a thin syrup. Add the mixed nuts to the pan and cook, without stirring, until the sugar caramelizes – this will take about 20 minutes and will happen suddenly. Remove the pan from the heat and stir the nuts well to make sure they are evenly coated in the caramel.

Add the nuts and any loose sugar crystals to the popcorn and stir through. This popcorn can be served warm or cold.

✳tip If you can only find salted roasted nuts, rinse the nuts in a colander and dry with paper towels before adding them to the sugar syrup.

Salt, when added to a rich caramel sauce, brings out the toffee flavour resulting in a lip-smackingly good popcorn coating. With added fudge pieces and mini marshmallows, this popcorn is a kitsch classic in the making!

Salted caramel popcorn

Heat the oil in a large lidded saucepan with a few popcorn kernels in the pan. When you hear the kernels pop, carefully tip in the rest of the kernels. Shake the pan over the heat until the popping stops. Take care when lifting the lid as any unpopped kernels may still pop from the heat of the pan. Tip the popcorn into a bowl, removing any unpopped kernels as you go.

For the caramel sauce, put the sugar and butter in a small saucepan set over gentle heat. Simmer until the butter has melted, the sugar has caramelized and you have a thick golden caramel sauce. Add the salt and stir again, taking care that the caramel does not burn. Add the cream gradually and heat, stirring all the time, until the sauce is thick and sticky. Pass through a sieve/strainer to remove any crystallized sugar pieces.

Pour the caramel over the popcorn and stir well so that each kernel is evenly coated. Set aside to cool for about 5 minutes. Sprinkle over the fudge and marshmallows and stir through. This popcorn can be served warm or cold.

*tip Mini mini marshmallows are available in supermarkets – they are the tiniest dainty marshmallows you can imagine . If you cannot find them, you can substitute the slightly larger mini marshmallows or chop large marshmallows into small pieces using scissors for equally good results.

1–2 tablespoons sunflower or vegetable oil

90 g/⅓ cup popcorn kernels

for the caramel sauce
75 g/⅓ cup caster/superfine sugar
40 g/2½ tablespoons butter
90 ml/⅓ cup double/heavy cream
¼ teaspoon sea salt

to serve
100 g/3½ oz. vanilla fudge, chopped into small cubes

40 g/1 cup mini mini marshmallows*

makes 1 bowl

When it comes to celebrating the 4th of July in America or a Royal event in Great Britain, this popcorn is the perfect accompaniment with its red, white and blue kernels. Alternatively you can use other colours to fit any theme of your choosing. Nice and simple, with just a little butter and sugar, this popcorn is perfect for any themed party.

red, white & blue popcorn

1–2 tablespoons sunflower or vegetable oil

90 g/⅓ cup popcorn kernels

80 g/5½ tablespoons butter

red and blue food colouring

60 g/5 tablespoons caster/superfine sugar

makes 1 large bowl

Heat the oil in a large lidded saucepan with a few popcorn kernels in the pan. When you hear the kernels pop, carefully tip in the rest of the kernels. Shake the pan over the heat until the popping stops. Take care when lifting the lid as any unpopped kernels may still pop from the heat of the pan. Divide the popcorn into three bowls, removing any unpopped kernels as you go.

Divide the butter between two small saucepans and heat gently until melted. Add a few drops of red food colouring to one pan and a few drops of blue to the other and stir. Pour the red butter over one of the bowls of popcorn and stir well so that the popcorn is evenly coated. Do the same with the blue butter. The third bowl remains white.

Leave the popcorn to set for about 20 minutes (or the colours will run together). After this time, add all the popcorn to a bowl, sprinkle with the sugar and stir to mix.

Serve in the bowl or divide between bags and seal with pretty, matching ribbon. This popcorn can be served warm or cold, but if you are sealing in bags, make sure the popcorn is cold before you do so.

Black truffle is one of life's finest luxuries. I remember once being served a truffle ice cream when I was young and being very disappointed that it tasted of garlic rather than chocolate! Since that time I must confess I have developed rather a passion for truffle and this popcorn recipe is a firm favourite. Truffle has been said to have aphrodisiac properties so be careful who you are with when you serve it!

black truffle popcorn

In a food processor, blitz the mushrooms to a fine powder and set aside.

Heat the oil in a large lidded saucepan with a few popcorn kernels in the pan. When you hear the kernels pop, carefully tip in the rest of the kernels. Shake the pan over the heat until the popping stops. Take care when lifting the lid as any unpopped kernels may still pop from the heat of the pan. Tip the popcorn into a bowl, removing any unpopped kernels as you go.

Melt the butter in a small saucepan set over medium heat and pour over the warm popcorn. Sprinkle over the mushroom powder and truffle salt and stir well so that the popcorn is evenly coated. This popcorn is best served warm.

*tip If you do not have truffle salt, simply drizzle a little truffle-infused oil over the popcorn and use regular sea salt instead.

20 g/¾ oz. dried porcini mushrooms

90 g/⅓ cup popcorn kernels

1–2 tablespoons sunflower or vegetable oil

70 g/5 tablespoons butter

1 teaspoon black truffle salt*

makes 1 large bowl

I have to confess, I love a margarita (or two!). There is something about the tang of lime mixed with salt and tequila that makes your tongue tingle. This may not be for everyone but if you love tequila then this is definitely the popcorn snack for you.

margarita popcorn

1–2 tablespoons sunflower or vegetable oil

90 g/⅓ cup popcorn kernels

70 g/5 tablespoons butter

grated zest and freshly squeezed juice of 3 unwaxed limes

80 g/scant ½ cup sugar

a few drops of green food colouring gel

1–2 tablespoons tequila

1 teaspoon flaked sea salt

makes 1 large bowl

Heat the oil in a large lidded saucepan with a few popcorn kernels in the pan. When you hear the kernels pop, carefully tip in the rest of the kernels. Shake the pan over the heat until the popping stops. Take care when lifting the lid as any unpopped kernels may still pop from the heat of the pan. Tip the popcorn into a bowl, removing any unpopped kernels as you go.

Melt the butter in a small saucepan set over gentle heat. Add the lime zest and juice and the sugar and simmer, stirring all the time, until the sugar has dissolved and you have a sticky syrup. Add a few drops of food colouring and stir to mix.

Pour the lime syrup over the popcorn and stir well so that all the kernels are evenly coated. Drizzle a little tequila over, then crush the sea salt between your fingers and sprinkle over the popcorn and stir again. This popcorn can be served warm or cold.

The Bloody Mary cocktail is always popular and is said to be the perfect hangover cure. Whilst I can't guarantee that this popcorn will cure a hangover, it is certainly a delicious snack anytime of the day! If you prefer, you can substitute tabasco sauce for the Worcestershire sauce and replace the celery salt with sea salt if you do not have any available.

bloody mary popcorn

Heat the oil in a large lidded saucepan with a few popcorn kernels in the pan. When you hear the kernels pop, carefully tip in the rest of the kernels. Shake the pan over the heat until the popping stops. Take care when lifting the lid as any unpopped kernels may still pop from the heat of the pan. Tip the popcorn into a bowl, removing any unpopped kernels as you go.

Melt the butter in a small saucepan set over medium heat and then pour over the warm popcorn. Sprinkle over the tomato powder, Worcestershire sauce and vodka, to taste. Season with salt and pepper and stir well so that all the kernels are evenly coated. This popcorn is best served immediately.

*tip Tomato powder is available from health food stores or on the internet. If you are not able to find any, you can use dried tomatoes (not those preserved in oil but air dried tomatoes). Remove them from the package and dry for about 1–2 hours in a very low temperature oven until they are completely dry then blitz to a fine powder in a blender.

1–2 tablespoons sunflower oil or vegetable oil

90 g/⅓ cup popcorn kernels

80 g/5½ tablespoons butter

20 g/3 tablespoons dried tomato powder*

1–2 tablespoons Worcestershire sauce

about 1 tablespoon vodka, to taste

celery salt and freshly ground black pepper

makes 1 large bowl

index